Minh's New Life

Story by Jay Sanders
Illustrations by Meredith Thomas

Minh could hear the gentle breathing of her two younger sisters as they slept peacefully beside her. She could hear the *swish-swish* of car wheels on the wet road outside, and the rumble of the bus heading north into the city. Minh wished she could go back to sleep, but the cold and her own fear kept her wide awake.

She had been in this new country only three weeks. It always seemed to be cold and rainy, and she couldn't understand the strange language that the teachers and students spoke at her new school. Whenever the teacher talked to her, she kept her head down, and stared at a book she did not understand. Her face was hidden behind her thick, black hair. No one spoke to her at recess—she sat alone.

Until a month ago, Minh had lived in Vietnam with her two sisters and her grandmother, where the country was green, warm, and familiar.

She remembered her grandmother's soft voice calling, "Get out of bed, sleepy head." How she missed her grandmother—her gentle hugs, her happy laughter, and her smile.

Minh could picture so clearly the women of her village working in the rice fields, their colorful clothes bright against an emerald sea.

Minh's father had left Vietnam two years earlier to begin a new life. He had written often, telling Minh and her sisters of this new country. He had worked very hard until, finally, he had been able to buy a small grocery store. He lived above the store in a busy street in a large city. At last, he had saved enough money to pay for Minh and her sisters to join him.

As the dawn light filled the room, Minh slid out of bed. She gazed out the window, afraid of what the new day would bring. When Minh had started school, her father and sisters had traveled with her each day. But today, she would have to go by herself for the first time! She felt very scared.

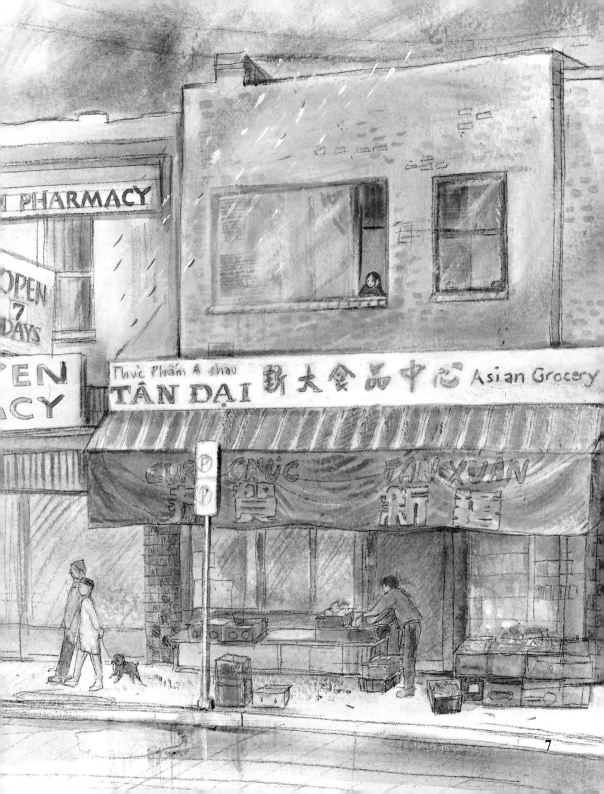

In the early morning light, Minh dressed in her school uniform. She took care not to disturb her sleeping sisters as she tiptoed quietly down the narrow wooden stairs to the store. Her father was already at work, sorting vegetables and polishing the different kinds of fruits he sold.

"Good morning, Father," Minh said.

He gave her a gentle smile and asked her if she would be okay today.

Minh nodded and returned a very tiny, but brave, smile. "I'll be fine," she said.

At eight o'clock, Minh gathered her coat and school backpack. Nervously, she waved goodbye to her father and sisters. The two little girls waved back as they stood close to their father's side.

Minh felt sick with fear. People walked briskly along the pavement, trying to avoid the puddles left by the recent downpour. No one seemed to notice the small figure walking alone toward the bus stop.

11

Minh stopped where her father had told her to wait. She glanced back toward the store —her father and sisters stood quietly, watching.

She could hear the sound of a city bus coming towards her. Minh looked up at the front of the bus. Fear gripped her—the bus did not have the 9 shape on the sign above the driver's window!

Should she catch this bus or wait for one with the number 9? She felt confused and so alone.

The woman beside Minh peered down at her. "Can I help you?" she asked.

Minh could not understand. Quickly, she turned away as if she hadn't heard.

The faded green bus rumbled on and another followed. Minh once again peered through the waiting crowd and looked for the number — it was number 9! Her heart skipped a beat as she waited her turn to enter the bus.

Some passengers glanced briefly at her as she moved toward the ticket machine. Her father had explained how the machine worked, but now she could not remember how to get the ticket. Should she put the money in first or press the buttons? The words on the machine meant nothing to her. She did not know what to do! The man behind her tapped his foot impatiently as he waited for her to buy a ticket.

Just as the first tear began to roll down her cheek, a small hand touched hers.

"Hello," said a young girl in Vietnamese. "I'll help you. My name is Lan and I go to the same school as you. I've seen you on the playground."

After Lan helped Minh to buy her ticket, they both went toward the back of the bus. Lan explained in Vietnamese that she and her mother had been in this country for one year. She could already speak English quite well and could read most of the books the other children in her class were reading. The two girls got off the bus at their stop and walked the rest of the way to school together.

Minh had made her first friend in her new home.